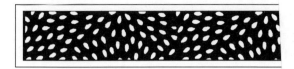

WILD ABOUT RICE

BY MARIE BIANCO

BARRON'S
New York • London • Toronto • Sydney

This book is for Frank who has always been there for me. Thanks for coming to my aid during computer glitches and especially when asked to try yet another dish.

All inquiries should be addressed to:
Barron's Educational Series, Inc.
250 Wireless Boulevard
Hauppauge, NY 11788

International Standard Book No. 0-8120-4263-8

Library of Congress Catalog Card No. 89-6840

Library of Congress Cataloging-in-Publication Data
Bianco, Marie.
　　Wild about rice/by Marie Bianco
　　p.　cm.
　　Includes index
　　ISBN 0-8120-4263-8
　　1. Cookery (Rice) I. Title.
TX809.R5B53　1989
641.6'318—dc20　　　　　　　　　　　89-6840
　　　　　　　　　　　　　　　　　　　　　CIP

Design by Milton Glaser, Inc.
Color photographs by Matthew Klein
Julie Gong, prop stylist
Ann Disrude, home economist

PRINTED IN HONG KONG

901　4900　987654321

CONTENTS

INTRODUCTION

Because I am a food writer, people are always asking me what foods are "hot." When I tell them to look for onion marmalade or fig confit, smoked venison or marinated goat cheese as new and exciting foods, I get that "Wow, isn't that something" expression and they're very happy. But if I tell them that rice will be the new and exciting food of the nineties, the result is an "I think she's been working too hard" stare.

People who care about their bodies are eating complex carbohydrates these days, so foods like pasta get high marks for being nutritionally sound. And I think the time may be right for another "pasta." Rice is that "new and different" complex carbohydrate that happens to be one of the world's oldest foods and the staple of half its population, eaten by every culture except perhaps, the Eskimos.

So this book is for those people who think that rice is used only in chicken soup, with Chinese takeout, and as rice pudding, as well as those who are passionate about paella, jambalaya, and risotto.

NOTE: In recipes where cooked rice is called for, long grain white, converted or brown rice may be used.

THE STORY OF RICE

The story of rice is as old as civilization itself. Some archeologists claim that rice has been consumed for over 5,000 years. Even today almost half the world's population uses rice as its number-one food. Annual per capita consumption worldwide is 143 pounds, but in southeast Asia it is as high as 300 pounds.

In this country the yearly rice consumption is less than 13 pounds per person. Consequently, although the United States grows only 2 percent of the world crop, it is one of the largest rice exporters. And this happened by accident about 300 years ago.

When a storm-battered ship took refuge in Charleston, South Carolina, harbor for repairs, the ship's captain gave a small amount of "Golde Seede Rice" (named for its color) to a local planter. The seed took root and flourished in the tidal marshlands of the Carolinas and Georgia. By 1700, colonists were producing more "Carolina Golde Rice" than there were ships to carry it to England. But rice cultivation is labor-intensive, and after the War Between the States the Carolina rice industry never recovered.

An enterprising farmer discovered that rice could be produced on the broad prairie of southwestern Louisiana and southeastern Texas, using the same methods employed for growing wheat. Ensuing mechanization revolutionized the rice industry in this country.

Around the turn of the century, rice-growing was attempted in Arkansas. It was so successful that people were attracted by the lure of cheap land and a bountiful harvest contributed to making Arkansas the country's leading rice-growing region. About 10 years later cultivation moved to California, and by 1920 it became a major rice-producing state.

Today, rice farms have sprung up in Mississippi and southern Missouri. The plant ranks sixth in production value of major field crops in the U.S., and about 66 percent of the crop is exported to more than 100 countries. Of the rice exported, two-thirds is long-grain, close to one-third is medium-grain, and the remainder is short-grain. The world's chief rice producers are China, India, Pakistan, Bangladesh, Burma, Thailand, Indonesia, Japan, the Philippines and Vietnam.

KINDS OF RICE

It's hard to believe that there are 40,000 different varieties of rice grown in the world today. Long-, medium- and short-grain types are the most popular in this country, but limited amounts of the waxy and aromatic varieties are also produced. All kinds of long, medium and short rice come in both white and brown varieties. Each of these rices is slightly different in appearance, and there are subtle taste differences as well. Nutritionally, however, all except waxy rice are about the same and can often be interchanged in recipes.

Long-grain rice is four to five times as long as it is wide; when the grains are cooked, they are separate and fluffy. An all-purpose rice, it is the most popular type in the United States today.

Medium rice is short and plump. Once cooked, the grains are moist and tender and have a tendency to cling together. It's good for risotto, molds and dessert, or when you want the rice to stick to itself.

Short-grain rice is rich in amylopectin, a starch that tenderizes the grains and at the same time makes them cling together. This type of rice is mostly sold in Oriental and Hispanic markets and is a favorite for sushi.

Waxy rice, also called sweet or glutinous rice, is short, plump and chalky white. Once it has been cooked, it loses its shape and becomes very sticky. Its starch and flour are used as a binder for frozen gravies and sauces because they do not break down after freezing and thawing.

Aromatic rices are long-grain types that give off an aroma of nuts or popcorn as they cook. A "wild pecan rice" and a "popcorn rice," both grown in Louisiana in limited quantities, are available mostly through mail order.

Another type of rice becoming more and more popular today is basmati, a curved, long-grain aromatic variety grown in India. A favorite with curries, basmati rice is frequently aged for a year to improve its flavor. A form of basmati rice called Texmati is successfully grown in Texas, and Wehani, a hybrid of basmati and brown rice with a nutty flavor and aroma, is cultivated in California.

Short, fat grains of arborio rice, from the Piedmont and Lombardy areas of Italy, are used chiefly for making risotto. Arborio rice is often sold in 1-pound cloth bags.

Although it is called rice, wild rice is not a true rice, but an aquatic grass grown in Minnesota, Canada and, most recently, California. It is chewy, dark brown and nutty in flavor. Though once very expensive, it has become much more affordable in the last few years thanks to expanded cultivation and the development of more efficient harvesting methods.

MILLING RICE

Milling, or processing rice from field to shelf, produces different products. Depending on the kind you choose, rice can take 45 minutes of simmering or be reconstituted in 5 minutes.

All rice starts out in the field as the same grain. White rice results after the grain's outer husk and bran layers are removed. It is often enriched with the nutrients that are thereby removed—iron, niacin and thiamine. One cup of raw white rice yields 3 cups after 15 to 18 minutes' cooking.

When just the outer husk is removed, the grain is called brown rice; the remaining layers of bran give it a nutty taste and a slight crunch. The bran also gives the rice its tan color, additional protein and nutrients. However, the barrier it forms makes more liquid and a longer cooking time necessary. Owing to the oil content of the bran, brown rice can become rancid if kept on the shelf too long, so uncooked brown rice should be stored in the refrigerator. One cup of brown rice yields 3 to 4 cups cooked.

Parboiled or "converted" rice is soaked, steamed, dried and then milled to remove the outer hull, causing a harder, more compact, shiny grain. The result is more nutritious but parboiled rice requires more liquid and a longer cooking time than plain rice. One cup of parboiled rice makes 3 to 4 cups cooked.

Precooked rice is enriched rice that has been milled, completely cooked and then dried. Upon the addition of boiling water, the grains rehydrate in just a few minutes. The most widely recognizable brand is Minute Rice.

RICE NUTRITION

It's hard to say anything bad about rice. It contains zero cholesterol, is low in fat and sodium, gluten-free and nonallergenic. Rice is a complex carbohydrate and is easy to digest. And it is almost always baby's first cereal.

Rice lacks one amino acid to make it a complete-protein food, but when served with beans, nuts or seeds it provides high-quality protein.

Although brown rice owes much of its nutritive content to its bran covering, white rice is enriched with the nutrients it loses during the milling process, so brown and white rice are almost even on the nutrition scoreboard. A ½ cup serving of white rice provides 82 calories; brown rice has 92 calories per serving.

TO RINSE OR NOT TO RINSE

Years ago, when rice was sold in open barrels or burlap bags, many shoppers rinsed rice as a way of cleaning it after it had been handled by shoppers or contaminated by insects. Even today, Asian cooks wash rice to an extreme. The Chinese may rinse rice in a strainer until the water runs clear, perhaps 10 minutes or longer. Japanese sometimes soak rice for several hours before cooking.

Today's rice comes in a sealed box or bag and does not require rinsing; in fact, rinsing enriched rice will wash away nutrients, many of which are water soluble. On the other hand, if you are buying imported rice and its former environment is uncertain, it is a good idea to give it a quick rinse under cold water just before cooking.

HOW TO COOK RICE

Every country has its own surefire way of cooking rice, and it all has to do with the ratio of rice to water.

The Chinese like to simmer it in twice the volume of water to rice, tightly covered. The Japanese boil it covered for 10 minutes, simmer it for 10 minutes and leave it off the heat for 10 minutes. In Singapore you are apt to find rice boiled in three to four times its volume of boiling water for 12 minutes, drained and dried out in the oven. Indians generally cook rice for 20 minutes before rinsing it in cold water. Italians cook rice like pasta, in large amounts of rapidly boiling water until it is al dente.

Here are five tips to remember when cooking rice:

Measure water and rice accurately.

Time the cooking.

The rice will triple or quadruple in volume, so use a large enough pot with a tight-fitting lid.

Do not remove the lid until the end of the cooking time.

If rice is not sufficiently done, return cover and cook a few minutes longer.

When rice is cooked, stir with a fork to allow steam to escape and to keep grains separate.

Here are some ways to cook rice on top of the stove. Adding ½ teaspoon salt and a tablespoon of butter or margarine to the pot are optional. Instead of water, you can add a lot of flavor to rice by cooking it in beef or chicken stock, the water left over from cooking vegetables, diluted tomato juice, unsweetened coconut milk or even clam broth, depending on what the rice is going to be served with.

The following times are estimates of how long rice should cook. The shape of the pot, how tightly the lid fits, how old the rice is, even altitude will affect the cooking time. If you always make your rice in the same pot, you will soon have it down to a science.

1 CUP UNCOOKED RICE	LIQUID	COOKING TIME	YIELD
Regular milled long-grain	1¾–2 cups	15–18 minutes	3 cups
Regular milled medium- or short-grain	1½ cups	15 minutes	3 cups
Brown	2–2½ cups	35–45 minutes	3 to 4 cups
Parboiled	2–2½ cups	20–22 minutes	3 to 4 cups

To cook rice in a conventional oven, combine rice with boiling liquid in the proportions given above, cover tightly and bake at 350°F (180°C) for 15 to 20 minutes longer than times given above. Fluff with fork.

To cook rice in the microwave oven, combine ingredients in above proportions, cover and cook on high power for 5 minutes or until boiling. Reduce power to 50 percent and cook for times listed above. Fluff with fork.

Automatic and non-automatic electric rice cookers are becoming more popular; they should be used following the manufacturer's instructions. They usually require less liquid than top-of-the-stove cooking.

To reheat rice, add 2 tablespoons liquid for each cup of rice. Cover and heat for about 5 minutes on top of the range, or for 1 minute in the microwave on high power.

As a side dish, plain rice can be enhanced by adding chopped scallions or parsley, stir-fried mushrooms, butter-browned almonds, some chopped fresh mint, sour cream and chives, fried onions, a dose of shredded cheddar cheese or a few raisins and toasted pine nuts.

Leftover rice can be added to meat loaf, soup, pancakes or salad, or scrambled with eggs.

STORAGE

Any form of white rice will keep indefinitely in a tightly closed container on the pantry shelf. Brown rice has a shelf life of six months, or much longer in the refrigerator.

Cooked rice will keep, tightly sealed, in the refrigerator for about a week, or frozen for up to six months.

OTHER USES FOR RICE

Rice flour *is used in commercial food processing, baking and cereals, and as a filler in meat products. When used in frozen foods, flour* *ground from waxy rice will stand up to the rigors of freezing and thaw-ing without causing defrosted gravies to separate as is sometimes the case with cornstarch. Because rice flour contains no gluten, those who are allergic to wheat can safely eat baked products made with it. Rice flour is sold at health food and specialty stores.*

Rice noodles *are popular in parts of Asia where no wheat is grown. They range from translucent rice sticks, which look like fishing line and expand the moment they are lowered into hot fat, to fat, chewy Chinese* chow fun *noodles.*

Rice bran *consists of the outer layers and germ directly beneath the seed's hull. With a nutty taste and crunchy texture, the bran is rich in protein and B-vitamins. Recent studies by the U.S. Department of Agriculture indicate that rice bran may be more effective than oat bran in lowering blood cholesterol.*

Sold in health food stores, rice bran can be sprinkled over hot or cold cereal, added to tunafish or egg salad or used as a crisp topping for ice cream. Substitute it for part of the bread in a meatloaf, or stir a few tablespoons into pancake or waffle batter and muffin or bread doughs.

NOTE: When a recipe calls for cooked rice, the cook can use plain or converted rice, or even brown rice.

Rice cereals *abound on supermarket shelves in a variety of shapes and tastes; puffed rice, Rice Krispies and Rice Chex are but a few.* ***Rice cakes,*** *made from compressed puffed rice, have also become popular.*

Rice oil, *extracted from rice bran, has a high smoking point, which makes it useful for deep-fat frying. It can also be used in salad dress-ings and mayonnaise. Since it is a plant product, the oil contains no* cholesterol. It is sold in Oriental and health food stores.

Rice vinegar is an Asian staple. It is a mild, clear vinegar used in making sushi rice as well as in salad dressings.

Beer brewing takes advantage of rice grains that have been broken during the milling process.

Rice wine is found in both China and Japan. Japanese saké is slightly sweet and most often served warm. (It is deceiving because it doesn't have an alcoholic taste but it can pack quite a wallop.) Mirin is a Japanese rice wine used only for cooking. Chinese rice wine, or shaoxing, is golden brown in color and has a rich, sweet mellow flavor.

CONVERSION TABLES

The weights and measure in the lists of ingredients and cooking instructions for each recipe are in both U.S. and metric units.

LIQUID MEASURES

The Imperial cup is considerably larger than the U. S. cup. Use the following table to convert to Imperial liquid units.

AMERICAN CUP (in book)	IMPERIAL CUP (adjusts to)
¼ cup	4 tablespoons
⅓ cup	5 tablespoons
½ cup	8 tablespoons
⅔ cup	¼ pint
¾ cup	¼ pint + 2 tablespoons
1 cup	¼ pint + 6 tablespoons
1¼ cups	½ pint
1½ cups	½ pint + 4 tablespoons
2 cups	¾ pint
2½ cups	1 pint
3 cups	1½ pints
4 cups	1½ pints + 4 tablespoons
5 cups	2 pints

Note: The Australian and Canadian cup measures 250 mL and is only slightly larger than the U. S. cup, which is 236mL. Cooks in Australia and Canada can follow the exact measurements given in the recipes, using either the U. S. or metric measures.

SOLID MEASURES

British and Australian cooks measure more items by weight. Here are approximate equivalents for basic items in the book.

	U. S. Customary	Imperial
Cheese (grated)	½ cup	2 oz.
	1 cup	4 oz.
Flour (sifted)	¼ cup	1¼ oz.
Herbs (fresh chopped)	¼ cup	¼ oz.
Meats (chopped)	1 cup	6–8 oz.
Nuts (chopped)	¼ cup	1 oz.
	½ cup	2 oz.
Rice	½ cup	4 oz.
	1 cup	8 oz.
	2 cup	16 oz.
Vegetables (chopped)	½ cup	2 oz.
	1 cup	4 oz.
	2 cups	8 oz.

OVEN TEMPERATURES

British cooks should use the following settings.

Gas mark	¼	2	4	6	8
Fahrenheit	225	300	350	400	450
Celsius	110	150	180	200	230

RICE IN SOUPS AND SALADS

HEARTY RICE AND BEAN SOUP

SERVES 8

INGREDIENTS

2 cups (450 g) dry black beans
5 cups (1.2 L) chicken stock
5 cups (1.2 L) water
2 smoked ham hocks
or a leftover ham bone
1 large onion, chopped
4 carrots, sliced
2 tablespoons chopped fresh
parsley
4 cloves garlic, minced
hot pepper sauce to taste
salt and freshly ground pepper
to taste
4 tablespoons (60 mL) dry
sherry
4 cups (300 g) cooked rice

Two 1-pound (450-g) cans of black beans can be substituted for the dry beans.

Wash beans and discard any foreign matter. Drain and place in large stockpot. Add cold water to cover the beans by 1 inch and soak overnight.

Drain off water and return beans to stockpot. Add chicken stock, water, ham hocks, onion, carrot, parsley and garlic and bring to boil. Reduce heat, cover and simmer, stirring occasionally, for about 2 hours or until beans are tender. Add hot pepper sauce, salt and pepper to taste. Puree half the soup in a food mill, food processor or blender and return to pot.

To serve, place ½ tablespoon sherry in bottom of each individual bowl. Fill with soup and top with ½ cup (35 g) rice.

Add a few sourdough rolls and an orange/red onion/lettuce salad and this soup will give you a whole meal.

In a large saucepan melt butter and cook zucchini, scallions and garlic until soft. Stir in chilies, cumin and oregano. Add chicken stock, beans and tomato and bring to boil. Reduce heat and simmer 15 minutes. Remove from heat, add potato and cheddar cheese and stir until cheese is melted. Season with salt and pepper. Ladle soup into serving bowls and top each with a mound of rice. Sprinkle with cilantro.

CHEESE AND RICE SOUP

SERVES 6

INGREDIENTS

1 tablespoon (15 g) butter
1 medium zucchini, chopped
¼ cup (30 g) sliced scallions
1 clove garlic, minced
2 tablespoons diced green chilies
¼ teaspoon ground cumin
¼ teaspoon dried oregano
5 cups (1.2 L) chicken stock
2 cups (480 g) cooked
pinto beans
1 tomato, seeded, chopped
1 medium russet potato,
cooked, riced
6 ounces (180 g) cheddar
cheese, shredded
salt and freshly ground pepper to
taste
3 cups (225 g) hot cooked rice
¼ cup (7 g) chopped cilantro

TURKEY SOUP

SERVES 8

INGREDIENTS

8 cups (2 L) water
turkey carcass
1 carrot, sliced
1 onion, halved
1 tomato, halved
2 stalks celery, halved
6 sprigs parsley
2 cups (120 g) sliced mushrooms
2 carrots, sliced
1 onion, coarsely chopped
2 stalks celery, chopped
1 tomato, seeded, chopped
1 large russet potato, peeled
1 teaspoon poultry seasoning
1 teaspoon fresh tarragon leaves,
chopped
salt and freshly ground pepper
to taste
2 cups (150 g) cooked rice
1 cup (175 g) chopped cooked
turkey

Ever wonder what to do with a turkey carcass? Why not make a nourishing soup for the Monday after a turkey celebration?

In a large stockpot combine water, turkey carcass (broken into pieces if it does not fit), 1 carrot, halved onion, tomato and celery, and parsley. Simmer for 1 hour. Remove carcass and discard vegetables. Pick off turkey meat and discard carcass.

Strain stock and return to clean pot. Add mushrooms, sliced carrot, chopped onion, celery and tomato, potato, poultry seasoning, tarragon, salt and pepper. Simmer for 1 hour.

Remove potato and puree. Stir into soup as a thickener. Stir in rice and cooked turkey.

Serve with a chilled white wine and a loaf of crusty bread for an easy summer supper. Don't forget some ice cream for dessert.

In a medium bowl combine rice, artichoke hearts, fontina and cheddar cheeses, ham, tomato, celery, olives and capers. Toss lightly.

Whisk together olive oil, vinegar, oregano, mustard, salt and pepper. Pour over rice mixture and toss lightly.

Arrange radicchio leaves on platter and top with salad.

Garnish with basil.

HAM AND CHEESE RICE SALAD

SERVES 6

INGREDIENTS

3 cups (225 g) cooked rice, cooled
1 6½-ounce (195 g) jar artichoke
hearts, drained, quartered
4 ounces (120 g) fontina cheese,
diced
4 ounces (120 g) cheddar cheese,
diced
4 ounces (120 g) Black Forest
ham, diced
1 large tomato, peeled, seeded,
coarsely chopped
2 stalks celery, diced
½ cup (115 g) sliced pitted
California olives
1½ tablespoons capers, rinsed
½ cup (120 mL) olive oil
2 tablespoons balsamic vinegar
pinch of dried oregano
½ teapoon Dijon mustard
salt and pepper to taste
radicchio leaves
4 basil leaves, chopped

HAWAIIAN TURKEY SALAD

SERVES 6

INGREDIENTS

3 cups (225 g) cooked brown
rice, cooled
2 cups (350 g) coarsely chopped
cooked turkey
1 cup (225 g) diced fresh
pineapple
1 7-ounce (210-g) can sliced
water chestnuts
1 Granny Smith apple, cored
and chopped
½ cup (60 g) chopped
macadamia nuts or pecans
salt and freshly ground pepper
to taste
½ cup (120 mL) plain yogurt or
mayonnaise
1 tablespoon pineapple juice
fresh spinach leaves
¼ cup (30 g) shredded coconut

Leftover turkey never tasted so good.

In a medium bowl combine rice, turkey, pineapple, water chestnuts, apple, macadamia nuts, salt and pepper. Toss lightly.

Combine yogurt or mayonnaise with pineapple juice. Pour over turkey mixture and toss lightly. Arrange on spinach leaves and sprinkle with coconut.

Jícama is a root vegetable similar in color and taste to water chestnuts. It is usually eaten raw, especially in Mexican dishes and salads.

In a large bowl combine rice with carrots, bell peppers and jícama.

Whisk together vegetable oil, sesame oil, vinegar, soy sauce, ginger, garlic and cayenne pepper. Toast sesame seeds in a small skillet over low heat. Add dressing and sesame seeds to rice and vegetables and toss gently. Chill for several hours.

SESAME BROWN RICE SALAD

SERVES 4 TO 6

INGREDIENTS

4 cups (300 g) cooked brown rice, cooled
2 carrots, very thinly sliced
1 red bell pepper, cut into thin strips
1 green bell pepper, cut into thin strips
½ cup (60 g) thinly cut jícama strips or water chestnuts
3 tablespoons vegetable oil
1 tablespoon sesame oil
2 tablespoons rice vinegar
2 tablespoons soy sauce
2 teaspoons grated fresh ginger
1 clove garlic, minced
⅛ teaspoon cayenne pepper
2 tablespoons sesame seeds

GAZPACHO SALAD

SERVES 4

INGREDIENTS

1½ cups (115 g) cooked rice,
cooled
2 large tomatoes, cut into wedges
1 cup (60 g) sliced mushrooms
¼ cup (30 g) sliced green bell
pepper
¼ cup (30 g) sliced red pepper
6 scallions, sliced
1 tablespoon chopped Italian
parsley
5 tablespoons olive oil
2 tablespoons red wine vinegar
1 clove garlic, minced
4 fresh basil leaves, chopped
salt and freshly ground pepper
to taste
fresh spinach leaves

Gazpacho is a soup eaten with a spoon, right? Not this one. It's a salad, and definitely eaten with a fork.

In a large bowl combine rice, tomatoes, mushrooms, bell peppers, scallions and parsley. Whisk together oil, vinegar, garlic, basil, salt and pepper. Pour over rice mixture and toss gently.

Serve on spinach leaves.

Opposite: Sushi (p. 26)

For those who say paella is too hearty for summer fare, here is a salad version.

Whisk together vinegar, olive oil, garlic, salt and pepper in a large bowl. Add rice and toss lightly. Add chicken, shrimp, tomato, onion, peas and olives and toss again. Serve on lettuce leaves.

PAELLA SALAD

SERVES 4

INGREDIENTS

3 tablespoons white wine vinegar
6 tablespoons olive oil
1 clove garlic, minced
salt and freshly ground pepper to taste
2 cups (150 g) cooked rice (cooked in chicken stock with a pinch of saffron)
1 cup (175 g) cubed cooked chicken breast
1 cup cooked shrimp, peeled and deveined
1 tomato, seeded and diced
1 small red onion, diced
½ cup (115 g) cooked green peas
⅓ cup (40 g) sliced California black olives
romaine lettuce leaves

Opposite: Paella Salad

SUSHI

SERVES 4 (MAKES 32 PIECES)

INGREDIENTS

2 cups (450 g) short-grain rice
2¼ cups (540 mL) water
⅓ cup (80 mL) rice vinegar
1 tablespoon sugar
½ teaspoon salt
4 sheets nori (toasted seaweed)

Sushi is vinegared rice; at sushi bars, it is usually wrapped in nori and stuffed. The rice is cooked with less water than usual so that it remains a bit chewy. Nori, shiitake mushrooms, pickled ginger, soy sauce and wasabi are available at Japanese markets.

Place rice in strainer and rinse until water runs clear; this may take 10 minutes. In a medium saucepan combine rice with water and let stand for 1 hour. Cover and bring to boil, then reduce heat and simmer for 12 minutes or until water is absorbed. Remove from heat, uncover, and drape a clean tea towel over the saucepan. Replace cover and let stand for 15 minutes.

In a very small nonaluminum saucepan combine rice vinegar, sugar and salt and heat over low heat until sugar is dissolved, stirring constantly.

Place cooked rice on a shallow platter and run a wooden spoon through it to separate grains. At the same time, cool it with a fan or hair dryer held in the other hand. Gradually add the vinegar mixture as you cool the rice.

To make sushi, lay a sheet of nori on a bamboo mat or heavy dishcloth. Spread 1 cup (75 g) of the sushi rice evenly on the nori, leaving a 1-inch (2.5 cm) strip uncovered at the upper edge.

Using a chopstick, make an indentation across the rice about ⅓ of the way from the bottom. Lay any of the fillings across the indentation. Starting with the edge closest to you, begin rolling nori tightly, using the mat or dishcloth to get started. Moisten the uncovered edge with water and seal. Wrap the mat around the rolled nori and shape it into a smooth cylinder. Remove mat and slice with a sharp knife into 8 equal portions. Stand on end and serve with pickled ginger, soy sauce and wasabi.

FILLINGS

each of the four combinations will fill 4 sheets of nori

8 imitation crabmeat legs, 4 slices avocado, 4 scallions

•

4 large steamed spinach leaves, 1 scrambled egg, 4 scallions

•

4 sliced sautéed shiitake mushrooms, 1 julienned cooked carrot

•

4 thinly sliced shrimp, thin slices of peeled cucumber

pickled ginger
Japanese soy sauce
wasabi (powdered green horseradish),
mixed with enough water to form a stiff paste

RICE WITH VEGETABLES, EGGS, AND CHEESE

RICE PILAF

SERVES 4

INGREDIENTS

2 teaspoons olive oil
1 chicken liver
2 tablespoons olive oil, divided
1 cup (115 g) chopped onion
2 tablespoons blanched slivered
almonds
2 tablespoons golden raisins
2 cups (450 g) long-grain rice
3 cups (720 mL) hot water
¼ teaspoon aniseed
½ teaspoon salt
¼ teaspoon cayenne pepper
pinch of saffron
2 tablespoons (30 g) butter,
melted
2 tablespoons diced pimiento

This rice pilaf was a favorite with shish kebab at Maxwell's Plum when the restaurant was located on Manhattan's Upper East Side.

In an ovenproof skillet heat 2 tablespoons olive oil and sauté chicken liver until cooked through. Remove liver and chop finely. Add 1 tablespoon oil and onion to skillet and sauté onion until lightly browned. Add almonds and sauté until browned.

Preheat oven to 350°F (180°C). Return liver to skillet. Add raisins, rice, water, aniseed, salt, cayenne, saffron and remaining 1 tablespoon oil. Bring to boil, stir and cover tightly. Bake until water is absorbed and rice is tender, about 45 minutes.

Spoon into a serving dish. Drizzle melted butter over top and garnish with pimiento.

Chinese Fried Rice is a good way to use up leftovers. Almost any meat, seafood or vegetable can be substituted for the ham, shrimp and peas.

Heat 1 tablespoon peanut oil in a large skillet. Add beaten eggs, swirl around pan, and cook until just set. Place a plate on top and, holding the pan and the plate together, flip them over. Slide the egg back into the pan and cook a few seconds longer. Remove egg and cool. Roll into a cylinder and slice in thin strips. Set aside. Wipe out skillet.

Heat 2 tablespoons peanut oil in same skillet and heat rice. Add ham, scallions, shrimp, water chestnuts, peas, mushrooms and soy sauce. Stir well to combine. Add reserved egg and heat through.

CHINESE FRIED RICE

SERVES 4

INGREDIENTS

3 tablespoons peanut oil, divided
2 eggs, lightly beaten
4 cups (300 g) cold cooked rice
½ cup (90 g) chopped ham
6 scallions, chopped
½ cup (90 g) chopped cooked shrimp
8 water chestnuts, chopped
½ cup (115 g) green peas, frozen or fresh
1 cup (70 g) chopped fresh mushrooms
¼ cup (60 mL) soy sauce

STUFFED EGGPLANT AND ZUCCHINI

SERVES 8

INGREDIENTS

2 small eggplants
2 medium zucchini
4 tablespoons olive oil, divided
1 cup (115 g) chopped onion
3 cloves garlic, chopped
1 cup (240 g) chopped seeded tomatoes
1 cup (75 g) cooked rice
2 tablespoons chopped Italian parsley
2 tablespoons chopped fresh basil
salt and freshly ground pepper to taste
1 cup (115 g) shredded mozzarella
½ cup (60 g) freshly grated Parmesan cheese

Serve these stuffed vegetables as a side dish with a roast or individually for lunch.

Preheat oven to 400°F (200°C). Cut eggplant and zucchini in half lengthwise. Brush cut sides with 2 tablespoons olive oil and place face down in a baking pan. Bake for 15 minutes. Keeping vegetables intact, remove flesh with spoon or melon baller, leaving ¼-inch (.5-cm) shells. Chop flesh and set aside. Retain oven temperature.

In a large skillet heat remaining 2 tablespoons olive oil and sauté onion and garlic until onion is limp. Stir in reserved eggplant and zucchini and cook for 10 minutes over low heat. Add tomatoes, rice, parsley, basil, salt, pepper and mozzarella. Mound mixture into vegetable shells. Sprinkle with Parmesan cheese and bake for 15 minutes.

Opposite: Stuffed Eggplant and Zucchini

Here is a Venetian classic. The best Parmesan cheese—Parmigiano-Reggiano—is expensive but its pungent flavor is worth it.

Melt butter in a large saucepan and sauté onion until transparent. Add rice and cook, stirring constantly, for 5 minutes, or until golden. Add chicken stock, cover and simmer for 18 minutes or until liquid is absorbed but mixture is still creamy.

Cook peas in a small amount of water until tender. Slice prosciutto into narrow strips.

Stir peas, prosciutto, salt, pepper and half the grated Parmesan into the rice. Transfer to a serving dish and sprinkle with remaining cheese. Serve at once.

RISI E BISI
(RICE AND PEAS)

SERVES 8

INGREDIENTS

½ cup (120 g) butter
1 cup (115 g) finely chopped onion
1½ cups (340 g) rice
3½ cups (850 mL) hot chicken stock
1½ cups (340 g) fresh or frozen green peas
2 ounces (60 g) thinly sliced prosciutto
salt and freshly ground black pepper to taste
1 cup (115 g) freshly grated Parmesan cheese

Opposite: Risi e Bisi

CURRIED BROWN RICE

SERVES 6

INGREDIENTS

2 tablespoons olive oil
1 cup (115 g) chopped onion
2 teaspoons curry powder, or to
taste
½ teaspoon ground ginger
¼ teaspoon ground cumin
¼ teaspoon turmeric
salt and freshly ground pepper
to taste
⅛ teaspoon cayenne pepper
1 cup (225 g) brown rice
2½ cups (600 mL) chicken stock
2 tablespoons raisins
2 tablespoons chopped almonds
1 tablespoon snipped chives

Some recipes call for cooking brown rice for an hour, but I find that a maximum of 40 minutes leaves it chewy yet tender.

In a large skillet or saucepan heat oil and sauté onion for 2 minutes. Add curry powder and cook 1 minute longer, stirring constantly. Add ginger, cumin, turmeric, salt, pepper, cayenne, brown rice and chicken stock and bring to boil. Reduce heat, cover and simmer for 40 minutes. Add raisins and almonds. Replace cover and set aside for 5 minutes. Sprinkle with chives.

If your budget can afford it, a few shavings of black truffle add a touch of elegance to this humble rice dish.

Melt 2 tablespoons butter in a heavy saucepan and sauté shallot and ginger 2 minutes, taking care not to burn them. Add remaining butter; when it melts, stir in rice. Cook, stirring constantly, until rice becomes opaque. Add carrot, orange zest and ½ cup (120 mL) hot stock. Stir mixture until stock is almost completely absorbed. Add remaining stock, ¼ cup (60 mL) at a time, stirring constantly until rice is al dente and creamy, about 20 minutes. Season with salt and pepper.

CARROT RISOTTO

SERVES 4

INGREDIENTS

4 tablespoons (60 g) butter, divided
1 shallot, finely chopped
1 tablespoon finely chopped fresh ginger
1 cup (225 g) arborio rice
1 cup (240 g) pureed cooked carrot
2 tablespoons (600 mL) finely chopped orange peel
2½ cups (60 mL) (approximately) hot chicken stock
salt and freshly ground pepper to taste

FENNEL RISOTTO

SERVES 4

INGREDIENTS

1 fennel bulb
4 tablespoons (60 g) butter,
divided
2 shallots, minced
2½ cups (480 to 600 mL)
chicken stock
1 cup (225 g) arborio rice
½ cup (60 g) freshly grated
Parmesan cheese
salt and freshly ground pepper to
taste

Raw fennel has a decidedly anise flavor, but once it is cooked, the taste mellows.

Trim stalks from fennel; discard. Cut bulb into quarters; discard hard core. Chop fennel coarsely. Melt 2 tablespoons butter in a heavy saucepan over low heat and cook shallots and fennel until tender. Remove and puree in a food processor.

Bring chicken stock to simmer.

In a heavy saucepan melt remaining butter. Add rice and cook over medium heat for 5 minutes or until opaque. Add ½ cup (120 mL) hot chicken stock to rice and stir constantly until liquid is almost absorbed. Continue to add ½ cup (120 mL) of hot chicken stock at a time, stirring until rice is creamy and tender. Remove rice from heat and stir in fennel mixture and Parmesan. Season with salt and pepper to taste.

Pistachio nuts add a nice crunch to this Greek specialty.

Heat 2 tablespoons olive oil and sauté onion until tender. Add rice and sauté 2 minutes, stirring constantly. Add water and bring to boil. Cover and simmer 15 minutes. Cool slightly, then add pistachios, parsley, tomato, 1 tablespoon lemon juice, mint, salt and pepper.

Soak grape leaves in warm water for 5 minutes; drain thoroughly and remove stems. With stem ends of leaves facing you, place 1 heaping tablespoon rice mixture on each leaf. Fold up stem end, fold in sides over rice and roll up from bottom. Arrange stuffed leaves in a large skillet or shallow saucepan. Add 3 tablespoons water and remaining olive oil and lemon juice. Place over high heat for 3 minutes. Cover tightly, reduce heat and simmer for 30 to 45 minutes or until rice is tender. Cool. Serve at room temperature.

PISTACHIO-STUFFED GRAPE LEAVES

MAKES 24 TO 30

INGREDIENTS

3 tablespoons olive oil, divided
1 small onion, minced
½ cup (110 g) rice
1 cup (240 mL) water
⅓ cup (40 g) shelled pistachio nuts, coarsely chopped
¼ cup (7 g) chopped fresh parsley
1 plum tomato, minced
2 tablespoons fresh lemon juice, divided
1 tablespoon chopped fresh mint
salt and freshly ground pepper to taste
24 to 30 grape leaves in brine
3 tablespoons water

CAJUN RED BEANS AND RICE

SERVES 6

INGREDIENTS

1 cup (225 g) dry kidney beans
1 quart (1 L) water
4 ounces (120 g) salt pork, diced
2 tablespoons vegetable oil
1 cup (115 g) chopped onion
½ cup (60 g) chopped green bell pepper
1 cup (115 g) chopped celery
2 cloves garlic, minced
¼ teaspoon dried oregano
¼ teaspoon dried thyme
1 8-ounce (240-g) can tomato sauce
8 ounces (240 g) pork sausage, cooked and crumbled
6 scallions, chopped
salt and pepper to taste
3 cups (225 g) hot cooked rice
hot pepper sauce

Red beans and rice is a famous New Orleans Monday-washday supper which makes use of Sunday's ham bone. This version calls for pork sausage in lieu of the bone.

Rinse beans and combine with water and salt pork in a large stockpot. Bring to boil and cook for 2 minutes. Remove from heat and set aside, covered, for 1 hour. Return to heat and simmer 45 minutes with cover ajar.

Heat oil in a medium skillet and sauté onion, green pepper, celery and garlic until onion is soft. Add vegetables to beans along with oregano, thyme and tomato sauce. Simmer 45 minutes, stirring occasionally. Stir in sausage and scallions and simmer 30 minutes longer or until beans are tender, adding water if necessary. Divide rice among 6 deep bowls and spoon beans on top. Add hot pepper sauce to taste.

No self-respecting Southerner would dream of beginning the New Year without a bowl of Hoppin' John.

In a stockpot combine ham hocks, onion, cayenne and cover with water. Cover and simmer for 1 to 1½ hours or until ham is tender.

Meanwhile, rinse blackeye peas. Combine peas and 6 cups (1.5 mL) water in a large saucepan. Boil 2 minutes, then remove from heat, cover and let stand 1 hour. Drain beans, discarding liquid.

Remove ham hocks from saucepan. Cut meat into small pieces, discarding rind and bone. Drain and discard onion from liquid. Measure liquid and add sufficient water to make 3½ cups (850 mL).

In large stockpot combine ham cooking liquid, ham, blackeye peas and rice and bring to boil. Reduce heat, cover and simmer for 20 to 30 minutes or until peas and rice are tender and liquid is absorbed. Season to taste with salt and pepper. Serve with hot pepper sauce.

HOPPIN' JOHN

SERVES 8

INGREDIENTS

2 to 3 meaty smoked ham hocks
1 cup (115 g) chopped onion
¼ teaspoon crushed cayenne
pepper
3½ cups (850 mL) water
2 cups (450 g) dried blackeye
peas
1½ cups (340 g) rice
salt and freshly ground pepper to
taste
hot pepper sauce

BLACK BEANS AND YELLOW RICE

SERVES 4

INGREDIENTS

4 ounces (120 g) bacon,
chopped
1 large onion, chopped
2 cloves garlic, chopped
1 cup (225 g) basmati rice or
long grain rice
¼ teaspoon turmeric
⅛ teaspoon cayenne pepper
2 cups (480 mL) water
1 tomato, seeded, chopped
1 small green bell pepper, diced
salt and freshly ground pepper to
taste
1 16-ounce (450-g) can black
beans, heated, drained

Serve this colorful dish with grilled pork chops or chicken sausage, or with a simple grilled fish.

Cook bacon in a large skillet over low heat until it begins to give off fat. Add onion and garlic and fry over medium heat for 2 minutes. Stir in rice, turmeric, cayenne and water and bring to boil. Reduce heat, cover and simmer for 15 minutes. Add tomato, green pepper, salt and pepper and cook, stirring once or twice, for 5 minutes or until rice is cooked and liquid is absorbed. Arrange rice on an oval platter and pile beans in the center. Serve at once.

Opposite: Ham and Cheese Rice Salad (p. 21)

Here's a good luncheon choice for using up August's tomato and zucchini harvest. A rice crust is a lower-calorie alternative to piecrust.

Preheat oven to 350°F (180°C). Combine rice, ¾ cup (90 g) mozzarella and 1 egg. Press into bottom and sides of a buttered 10-inch (25-cm) deep pie pan. Arrange zucchini and tomato over crust.

Melt butter in a small saucepan and sauté onion until tender. Blend in flour. Stir in ½ cup (120 mL) milk and cook, stirring constantly, until mixture is thick and bubbly. Remove from heat. Beat remaining milk and eggs with salt, pepper and basil. Stir in onion mixture and pour over vegetables in crust. Bake for 30 minutes. Sprinkle with remaining mozzarella and Parmesan cheeses. Return to oven for about 10 minutes or until custard is set and cheese is bubbly. Let stand 10 minutes before serving.

ZUCCHINI-TOMATO QUICHE WITH RICE CRUST

SERVES 6

INGREDIENTS

3 cups (225 g) cooked rice
1¼ cups (145 g) shredded mozzarella cheese, divided
4 eggs, divided
1 zucchini, halved and thinly sliced
1 tomato, chopped
2 tablespoons (30 g) butter
¾ cup (90 g) chopped onion
2 tablespoons all-purpose flour
¾ cup (180 mL) milk, divided
salt and freshly ground pepper to taste
2 tablespoons chopped fresh basil
3 tablespoons grated Parmesan cheese

Opposite: Zucchini-Tomato Quiche

PEPPERONI PIZZA WITH THREE CHEESES

SERVES 4

INGREDIENTS

2 cups (115 g) cooked rice
1 egg, beaten
½ cup (60 g) shredded
mozzarella cheese
1 cup (240 mL) tomato sauce
¼ teaspoon dried basil
½ teaspoon chopped garlic
¼ teaspoon dried oregano
2 tablespoons grated Parmesan
cheese
1 cup (115 g) shredded
mozzarella cheese
2 ounces (60 g) pepperoni
sausage, thinly sliced
½ cup (30 g) sliced mushrooms
1 tablespoon chopped Italian
parsley

And you thought pizza had to be made with a bread dough crust.

Preheat oven to 400°F (200°C). In a bowl combine rice, egg and mozzarella cheese. Press into a buttered 12-inch (30-cm) pizza pan. Bake for 4 minutes. Spread tomato sauce over rice crust and sprinkle with basil, garlic, oregano and Parmesan cheese. Layer with half the mozzarella and the pepperoni and mushrooms. Top with remaining mozzarella and parsley. Bake for 8 to 10 minutes or until mozzarella is bubbly.

Heat oil in a skillet and sauté mushrooms, shallots and garlic until limp. Stir in spinach and rice and cook for 2 minutes. Stir in flour and set aside.

Preheat oven to 375°F (190°C). In a bowl beat eggs with ricotta, Parmesan, nutmeg, salt and pepper. Stir in mozzarella.

Roll out half the pastry into a 13-inch (32.5-cm) circle and line a 10-inch (25-cm) deep pie plate. Trim pastry even with rim. Prick with a fork. Brush with egg white; bake 10 minutes. Retain oven temperature.

In partially baked crust layer one-half the spinach mixture, one-half the cheese mixture, the remaining spinach mixture, red peppers and remaining cheese mixture.

Roll remaining pastry into a 12-inch (30-cm) circle. Cover filling with pastry, trimming edge to ½ inch (1 cm). Fold top crust under and flute edge. Bake for 45 minutes or until crust is golden brown.

RICE AND VEGETABLE PIE

SERVES 6

INGREDIENTS

2 tablespoons olive oil
1 cup (60 g) sliced mushrooms
2 shallots, chopped
2 cloves garlic, minced
1 10-ounce (300-g) package frozen chopped spinach,
cooked and squeezed dry
1 cup (75 g) cooked brown rice
1 tablespoon all-purpose flour
4 eggs, slightly beaten
2 cups (450 g) ricotta cheese
¼ cup (30 g) grated Parmesan cheese
¼ teaspoon nutmeg
salt and pepper to taste
4 ounces (120 g) mozzarella cheese, sliced
pastry for 10-inch (25-cm) double-crust pie
1 egg white, slightly beaten
1 2-ounce (60-g) jar roasted red peppers,
drained and cut into strips

JALAPEÑO RICE SOUFFLÉ

SERVES 6

INGREDIENTS

⅓ cup (80 g) butter
6 tablespoons all-purpose flour
1 cup (240 mL) milk, divided
6 ounces (180 g) Monterey Jack
cheese, shredded
2 to 3 canned green chilies,
chopped
salt and freshly ground pepper to
taste
6 eggs, separated
2 cups (150 g) cooked rice

Rice lends an interesting texture to this soufflé.

In a medium saucepan melt butter and blend in flour. Add ¾ cup (180 mL) milk and cook over medium heat, stirring constantly, until sauce is thick and bubbly. Remove from heat, add cheese and chilies, and stir until cheese is melted. Cool slightly. Season with salt and pepper.

Preheat oven to 325°F (165°C). Beat egg yolks with remaining milk. Stir egg mixture and rice into cheese mixture. Beat egg whites until stiff but not dry. Carefully fold into rice mixture. Turn into an ungreased 2-quart (2.5-L) soufflé dish. Bake for 40 to 50 minutes or until knife inserted 1 inch (2.6 cm) from center comes out clean. Serve immediately.

Serve these tasty pancakes as a light lunch or as a side dish with other Oriental dishes.

In a medium bowl combine bean sprouts, scallions, green pepper, cabbage, mushrooms and rice. Toss lightly. Add eggs, soy sauce, salt (if necessary) and pepper and mix gently.

Heat griddle and oil lightly. Place ½ cup (120 mL) mixture at a time on hot griddle and gently pat with spatula into 4-inch (10-cm) circles. Cook until lightly brown on both sides.

To make sauce, mix cornstarch with a few tablespoons of the chicken stock in a saucepan. Stir in remaining stock and cook over medium heat until thickened. Stir in soy sauce and sesame oil. Pour sauce over pancakes and sprinkle with scallions.

EGG FOO YONG WITH CHINESE SAUCE

MAKES 15 PANCAKES

INGREDIENTS

3 cups (150 g) bean sprouts
½ cup (60 g) sliced scallions
2 tablespoons finely chopped green bell pepper
1 cup (50 g) finely shredded cabbage
½ cup (35 g) chopped mushrooms
2 cups (150 g) cooked brown rice
8 eggs, lightly beaten
2 tablespoons soy sauce
salt and freshly ground pepper to taste
vegetable oil
1 tablespoon corn starch
2 cups (360 mL) chicken stock
2 tablespoons soy sauce
1 teaspoon sesame oil
2 chopped scallions for garnish

ZUCCHINI AND ITALIAN SAUSAGE FRITTATA

SERVES 6

INGREDIENTS

8 ounces (240 g) Italian sausage
1 medium zucchini, shredded
2 tablespoons finely chopped red
bell pepper
½ cup (60 g) finely chopped
onion
1 clove garlic, minced
4 eggs, slightly beaten
½ cup (120 mL) half-and-half or
light cream
¼ cup (30 g) grated Parmesan
cheese
salt and freshly ground white
pepper to taste
¼ teaspoon nutmeg
1 cup (115 g) shredded Swiss
cheese
3 cups (225 g) cooked rice

Avoid using large zucchini; they have lots of seeds. If you must, cut them in half and scrape out the seeds with a spoon and discard.

Remove casing from sausage and cook sausage in a medium skillet until it loses its pink color, stirring to break up meat. Pour off all but 1 tablespoon fat. Add zucchini, red pepper, onion and garlic and cook until tender.

Preheat oven to 350°F (180°C). Combine eggs, half-and-half, Parmesan cheese, seasonings and ½ cup (60 g) shredded Swiss cheese. Stir sausage and egg mixtures into rice in a large bowl and mix well. Turn into a buttered shallow 2-quart (2-L) casserole. Sprinkle with remaining cheese. Bake until set, about 30 minutes.

A spinoff of pasta alla carbonara, this can be served either as a first course or by itself along with an endive, radicchio and arugula salad.

Heat butter and oil in a large skillet over medium heat. Add ham and sauté until slightly browned. Stir in rice, bacon, cheese, parsley, pepper and cream. Stir until mixture is creamy and thoroughly heated.

RICE ALLA CARBONARA

SERVES 6

INGREDIENTS

2 tablespoons (30 g) butter
1 tablespoon olive oil
8 ounces (240 g) cooked ham, julienned
3 cups (225 g) cooked rice
8 ounces (240 g) sliced bacon, cooked crisp, crumbled
⅔ cup (80 g) freshly grated Parmesan cheese
2 tablespoons chopped Italian parsley
½ teaspoon freshly ground black pepper
¾ cup (180 mL) heavy cream

RICE WITH FOUR CHEESES

SERVES 6

INGREDIENTS

3 cups (225 g) cooked rice
½ cup (60 g) freshly grated
Parmesan cheese
½ cup (60 g) diced ricotta salata
1 cup (115 g) shredded
mozzarella cheese
½ cup (60 g) shredded fontina
cheese
½ cup (60 g) diced pepperoni
3 eggs, slightly beaten
1½ cups (360 mL) milk
salt and freshly ground pepper to
taste
¼ cup (30 g) fine dry bread
crumbs
2 tablespoons olive oil

Ricotta salata is aged fresh ricotta cheese. There really is no substitute, so if you cannot locate it, omit it and make rice with three cheeses.

Preheat oven to 350°F (180°C). Combine rice in a bowl with Parmesan, ricotta salata, mozzarella, fontina and pepperoni, and toss lightly. Add eggs, milk, salt and pepper and toss lightly. Transfer to a buttered shallow 1½-quart (1.5-L) baking pan.

In a small dish combine breadcrumbs and olive oil. Sprinkle over rice mixture. Bake for 35 to 40 minutes or until set.

Opposite: Cajun Red Beans and Rice (p. 38)

Arancini *means "little oranges," which is exactly what these stuffed fried rice balls look like. They are common street food in the small towns of Sicily.*

In a heavy saucepan bring water to boil. Add rice, salt and 2 tablespoons olive oil. Cover and simmer for 20 minutes. Add remaining oil and cheese and mix well. Cool slightly.

To form balls, place 2 tablespoons rice in palm of hand and form a depression in the center. Fill with a tablespoon of filling. Cover with 2 more tablespoons rice and press into ball.

Dip rice balls into beaten egg, then into breadcrumbs. Refrigerate 30 minutes.

Pour vegetable oil into a deep saucepan to depth of 3 inches (7.5 cm). Fry arancini until golden brown, turning several times. Drain well. Serve warm or at room temperature.

ARANCINI

MAKES 24

INGREDIENTS

4 cups (1 L) water
1 pound (450 g) long-grain rice
2 teaspoons salt
6 tablespoons olive oil, divided
½ cup (60 g) freshly grated
Parmesan cheese
Ricotta or meat filling
(see next page)
1 egg, slightly beaten
fine dry breadcrumbs
vegetable oil for deep-frying

Opposite: Chinese Fried Rice (p. 31)

RICOTTA FILLING

MAKES ABOUT 4 CUPS (950 G)

1 15-ounce (450-g) container
ricotta cheese
8 ounces (240 g) mozzarella
cheese, shredded
4 ounces (120 g) prosciutto,
chopped
1 egg, slightly beaten
2 tablespoons finely chopped
Italian parsley
salt and freshly ground pepper to
taste

MEAT FILLING

1 tablespoon olive oil
½ pound ground lean beef
½ cup tomato sauce
1 tablespoon chopped fresh basil
½ cup finely chopped fresh
mushrooms
½ cup green peas, fresh or frozen

In a medium bowl combine ricotta, mozzarella, prosciutto, egg, parsley, salt and pepper. Mix well.

Heat olive oil in medium skillet and cook beef until it loses its redness. Pour off any fat. Stir in sauce, basil, mushrooms and peas. Cook 10 minutes over low heat. Cool.

Stuff a chicken or small turkey with this dressing or bake it in its own dish. To toast pine nuts, place them in a 350°F (180°C) oven for 10 to 15 minutes, shaking the pan two or three times until the nuts become lightly tanned.

Preheat oven to 350°F (180°C). Melt butter in a small skillet over medium heat and sauté onion and celery until tender. Combine with rice, pine nuts, parsley, poultry seasoning, salt, pepper, chicken stock and egg and mix well. Transfer mixture to a buttered 2½ quart (2.5-L) baking dish and bake for 30 minutes.

PIGNOLI RICE DRESSING

SERVES 6

INGREDIENTS

1 tablespoon (15 g) butter
⅓ cup (40 g) chopped onion
⅓ cup (40 g) chopped celery
3 cups (225 g) cooked brown rice
¼ cup (30 g) pine nuts, toasted
1 tablespoon chopped fresh parsley
¾ teaspoon poultry seasoning
¼ teaspoon salt
⅛ teaspoon freshly ground black pepper
1 cup (240 mL) chicken stock
1 egg, beaten

APPLE PECAN RICE DRESSING

SERVES 6

INGREDIENTS

8 ounces (240 g) bulk pork sausage
½ cup (60 g) chopped celery
¼ cup (30 g) chopped onion
3 cups (225 g) cooked rice
1 Granny Smith apple, cored and chopped
½ cup (60 g) chopped pecans
½ teaspoon dried sage
salt and freshly ground pepper to taste
½ cup (120 mL) chicken stock

Regardless of whether you call it dressing or stuffing, this one goes exceptionally well with roast pork.

Preheat oven to 350°F (180°C). In a large skillet cook sausage, celery and onion over medium heat, stirring to crumble meat. Drain off fat. Transfer to a bowl and add rice, apple, pecans, sage, salt, pepper and chicken stock. Mix well. Place mixture in a buttered 2½ quart (2.5-L) baking dish and bake for 25 minutes.

RICE WITH SEAFOOD

CATFISH FILLETS STUFFED WITH WILD RICE AND WALNUT SAUCE

SERVES 6

INGREDIENTS

4 slices bacon, chopped
1 cup (70 g) chopped fresh mushrooms
1 small onion, minced
1 stalk celery, minced
2 cups (150 g) cooked wild rice
salt and freshly ground pepper to taste
2 pounds (900 g) catfish or flounder fillets

WALNUT SAUCE

3 tablespoons (45 g) butter
1 cup (60 g) sliced fresh mushrooms
3 scallions, chopped
3 tablespoons all-purpose flour
½ teaspoon dry mustard
¼ teaspoon dried tarragon
2 cups (480 mL) half-and-half or light cream
¼ cup (30 g) chopped toasted walnuts

Catfish fillets are available in most fish stores and supermarkets. Toast walnuts in a 350°F (180°C) oven for 10 to 15 minutes.

To make stuffing, fry bacon in a skillet until lightly browned. Remove and set aside. Sauté mushrooms, onion and celery in bacon fat until tender. Stir in bacon and wild rice. Season with salt and pepper.

Preheat oven to 400°F (200°C). Lay fillets skin side up. Spread ¼ cup (60 g) stuffing and roll up. Place remaining stuffing on bottom of greased 2-quart (2-L) baking pan. Arrange on stuffing. Cover dish with lightly buttered waxed paper and bake for 15 minutes or until fish is opaque.

To make sauce, melt butter and sauté mushrooms and scallions until tender. Stir in flour, mustard, tarragon, and salt and pepper to taste. Add half-and-half gradually and cook until thickened, stirring constantly. Pour sauce over fillets and sprinkle with walnuts.

Kedgeree originated in Britain by way of India, hence the touch of curry and red pepper.

Chop egg whites; mash yolks with fork.

Place fish in a single layer in skillet. Cover with cold water and bring to boil. Reduce heat, cover and poach for 10 minutes. Drain and break fish into chunks, discarding any bones and skin.

Melt butter in a medium skillet and sauté onion and curry until onion is opaque. Stir in chopped egg white, rice, salt and cayenne pepper. Carefully fold in fish. Transfer to serving platter and sprinkle with egg yolk and parsley.

KEDGEREE

SERVES 6

INGREDIENTS

4 hard-cooked eggs, separated
1 pound (450 g) smoked haddock or cod
¼ cup (60 g) butter
1 cup (115 g) chopped onion
¼ teaspoon curry powder, or to taste
2 cups (150 g) hot cooked rice
salt to taste
¼ teaspoon cayenne pepper
chopped parsley for garnish

BAKED STUFFED TROUT

SERVES 6

INGREDIENTS

6 whole boned trout
2 tablespoons (30 g) butter
1 cup (60 g) sliced mushrooms
6 ounces (180 g) imitation
crabmeat, flaked
1 cup (75 g) cooked rice
1 tablespoon snipped fresh
chives
1 tablespoon chopped fresh dill
1 teaspoon grated lemon peel
salt and freshly ground pepper
to taste
1 tablespoon fresh lemon juice
1 tablespoon olive oil
¼ cup (60 mL) dry white wine

Whole boned trout are sold by most fishmongers. Serve these with stir-fried broccoli, yellow bell peppers and cherry tomatoes. Add a bottle of dry white wine, some dinner rolls, and a chocolate dessert and you're ready for company.

Pat fish dry. Open fish flat and arrange skin side down on an oiled 10 × 15-inch (25 × 37.5-cm) jelly roll pan.

Melt butter in a large skillet and sauté mushrooms until they are tender and all liquid has evaporated. Remove from heat and add crabmeat, rice, chives, dill, lemon peel, salt and pepper.

Preheat oven to 375°F (190°C). Brush fish cavities lightly with lemon juice. Spoon stuffing into cavities and skewer closed. Brush fish with oil. Pour wine into pan.

Bake for 10 minutes or until fish just flakes when tested with fork.

Many of the mussels you buy today are cultivated on mussel farms.

In a large stockpot bring wine, clam broth, onion, parlsey and bay leaf to boil. Add mussels, cover and steam until mussels open, about 5 minutes; discard any that do not open. Strain mussels, reserving liquid. Remove meat and discard shells and vegetables.

Soak saffron in 2 tablespoons reserved mussel liquid. Bring 2 cups (500 mL) reserved liquid to simmer. Heat half-and-half in second pan.

In a heavy saucepan melt butter and sauté onion and garlic for 5 minutes. Add rice and cook until opaque. Add ½ cup (120 mL) mussel liquid and cook, stirring constantly, until mixture absorbs almost all the liquid. Add remaining mussel liquid ½ cup (120 mL) at a time, then the half-and-half ½ cup (120 mL) at a time, stirring constantly, until rice is tender and creamy, about 20 minutes. Stir in reserved mussels, saffron mixture and Parmesan. Season with pepper.

MUSSEL RISOTTO

SERVES 6

INGREDIENTS

1 cup (240 mL) dry white wine
1 cup (240 mL) bottled clam broth
1 small onion, chopped
4 sprigs Italian parsley
1 small bay leaf
4 pounds (1.8 kg) mussels, scrubbed
a few threads of saffron
1 cup (240 mL) half-and-half or light cream
¼ cup (60 g) butter
1 onion, chopped
4 cloves garlic, minced
1½ cups (340 g) arborio rice
½ cup (60 g) freshly grated Parmesan cheese

BASQUE-STYLE RICE

SERVES 4

INGREDIENTS

3 dozen mussels, scrubbed
2 cups (480 mL) clam broth or
fish stock
2 tablespoons olive oil
1½ cups (340 g) long-grain rice
3 cups (720 mL) water
1 green bell pepper, sliced
2 cloves garlic, minced
4 ounces (120 g) chorizo
sausage or pepperoni, sliced
Spanish paprika
8 ounces (240 g) shrimp, shelled
lemon wedges, for garnish

The Basque people live in an area that overlaps Spain and France. Their foods reflect both cultures.

Place mussels in a large stockpot with clam broth and olive oil. Bring to boil, reduce heat, cover tightly and steam for about 5 minutes or until mussels open. Strain and reserve liquid. Discard mussels that do not open.

Preheat oven to 350°F (180°C). In a saucepan combine rice with water and bring to boil. Cook 8 minutes; rinse rice under cold water and drain. Combine rice in a buttered shallow baking dish with green pepper, garlic, chorizo and paprika. Stir in 2 cups (480 mL) mussel cooking liquid, adding water if necessary. Cover with a sheet of foil and a tight lid. Bake for 25 minutes.

Cover shrimp with water and simmer until pink. Drain well.

Spread rice on a large serving platter and arrange mussels and shrimp on top. Garnish with lemon wedges.

Red and green peppers lend color to saffron rice, studded with plump scallop morsels.

Season scallops with salt and pepper. Heat oil in large skillet over high heat and sauté scallops until golden brown. Remove and keep warm.

Sauté bell peppers, onion and garlic in same skillet for 2 minutes. Add tomatoes and cook, uncovered, on medium heat for 1 minute, stirring occasionally. Stir in rice, paprika, saffron, wine, clam broth, salt and pepper and bring to boil. Reduce heat, cover and simmer for 15 to 20 minutes or until rice is tender and liquid is absorbed. Stir in scallops. Transfer to a serving dish and sprinkle with parsley.

SCALLOPS AND RICE

SERVES 4

INGREDIENTS

1 pound (450 g) sea scallops, halved
salt and freshly ground pepper to taste
2 tablespoons olive oil
1 green bell pepper, chopped
1 red bell pepper, chopped
1 onion, chopped
2 cloves garlic, minced
2 tomatoes, seeded, chopped
1 cup (225 g) rice
1 tablespoon paprika
pinch of saffron
1 cup (240 mL) dry white wine
1 cup (240 mL) clam broth
2 tablespoons chopped Italian parsley

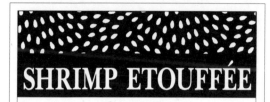

SHRIMP ETOUFFÉE

SERVES 4

INGREDIENTS

6 tablespoons (90 g) butter,
divided
¼ cup (30 g) all-purpose flour
1 large onion, chopped
½ cup (60 g) chopped green bell
pepper
½ cup (60 g) chopped celery
4 cloves garlic, minced
salt to taste
¼ teaspoon freshly ground black
pepper
¼ teaspoon cayenne pepper
1 teaspoon fresh lemon juice
6 scallions, chopped
2 tablespoons chopped parsley
1 cup (240 mL) clam broth
1½ cups (360 mL) water
1 pound (450 g) shelled shrimp
1 tablespoon paprika
4 cups (300 g) cooked rice

Etouffée is the Cajun version of stew. It begins with a roux made by cooking flour and butter together until the flour darkens. The result is a rich brown sauce with lots of flavor.

Melt 4 tablespoons (60 g) butter in a small, heavy cast iron skillet. Add flour and cook over medium heat, stirring constantly with a wooden spoon, until mixture is medium brown; this will take about 20 minutes.

In a separate skillet melt remaining 2 tablespoons (30 g) butter and sauté onion, green pepper, celery and garlic until onion is tender. Add the flour/butter mixture, salt, black and cayenne pepper, lemon juice, scallions and parsley. Slowly add broth and water. Simmer 15 minutes. Add shrimp and paprika and simmer 15 minutes longer. Serve in bowls, topping with a mound of rice.

This seafood mixture can also be baked at 350°F (180°C) in a loaf pan for 45 minutes or until internal temperature is 140°F. When it is removed from the oven, weigh it down in the refrigerator for several hours and pour off any liquid before slicing.

Combine fish and egg whites in food processor and process until smooth. With machine running, slowly add cream, lemon juice, tarragon and salt. Transfer to large bowl.

Shell shrimp, reserving shells. Combine shrimp, salmon and scallops in food processor and chop coarsely using on/off turns. Add rice and shrimp mixture to cream mixture. Chill.

Form ½ cup (120 g) of mixture into sausage shape about 5 inches (12.5 cm) long. Wrap in plastic wrap; twist ends and fold under. Repeat with remaining mixture. Bring water to simmer in a large skillet. Add sausages and poach for 15 minutes. Remove and cool for 5

SEAFOOD SAUSAGE WITH SHRIMP SAUCE

SERVES 6 (MAKES 12 SAUSAGES)

INGREDIENTS

1 pound (450 g) skinless white
fish fillets, cubed
4 egg whites
1 cup (240 mL) heavy cream
1 tablespoon fresh lemon juice
1 tablespoon chopped fresh
tarragon or 1 teaspoon
dried tarragon
1 teaspoon salt
8 ounces (240 g) unshelled
shrimp
4 ounces (120 g) salmon, cubed
4 ounces (120 g) scallops
1 cup (75 g) cooked rice
2½ quarts (2.5 L) water

SAUCE

1 cup (240 g) butter
reserved shrimp shells
½ cup (120 mL) dry white wine
¼ cup (60 mL) fresh
lemon juice
2 tablespoons minced shallot
¼ cup (60 mL) heavy cream
1 tablespoon chopped fresh
tarragon or 1 teaspoon dried
tarragon

minutes before unwrapping.

For sauce:
Melt butter in a small skillet and sauté shrimp shells until pink. Cool, then chop in food processor. Strain butter, discarding shells. Refrigerate butter. Bring wine, lemon juice, shallot, cream and tarragon to boil in a nonaluminum saucepan and boil until reduced to 2 tablespoons. Remove from heat and whisk in 2 tablespoons shrimp butter. Return pan to low heat and whisk in remaining shrimp butter a tablespoon at a time. Serve sauce over sausage.

Paella is traditionally made in a paellero but any large, deep casserole with a tight lid should do. There is no one recipe for this dish; each region of Spain claims its own as the best. This one is from Basque country.

Cook bacon in a large skillet until fat is rendered. Add rabbit and brown on all sides in bacon fat. Reduce heat and cook rabbit for 20 minutes. Remove and set aside.

Add olive oil to pan and place over medium heat. Add rice and stir until golden. Transfer rice to large paella pan, casserole or roasting pan. Stir in peas, onion, chorizo, garlic and red and green peppers. Push rabbit pieces down into the mixture. Heat chicken stock and stir in saffron, salt and pepper.

Preheat oven to 350°F (180°C). Place paella pan on oven rack and pour in chicken stock. Cover tightly and bake for 20 minutes. Remove cover and stir mixture. Replace cover and bake 15 minutes longer. Arrange mussels,

BASQUE PAELLA

SERVES 4

INGREDIENTS

4 ounces (120 g) slab bacon, coarsely chopped
1 small rabbit or chicken cut into 8 pieces
2 tablespoons olive oil
1½ cups (340 g) long-grain rice
1 cup (225 g) fresh or frozen green peas
1 large Spanish onion, chopped
4 ounces (120 g) chorizo sausage or pepperoni, sliced
3 cloves garlic, minced
1 red bell pepper, cut into 1-inch (2.5-cm) squares
1 green bell pepper, cut into 1-inch (2.5-cm) squares
4 cups (1 L) chicken broth
generous pinch of saffron
salt and freshly ground pepper to taste
16 mussels, scrubbed
8 ounces (240 g) shrimp, shelled

INGREDIENTS
(CONTINUED)

1 pound (450 g) firm-fleshed
white fish fillets
(cod, haddock, etc.), cut into
1-inch (2.5-cm) cubes
½ cup (60 g) pitted green olives
½ cup (60 g) pitted black olives

shrimp, fish and olives on top of rice.
Again cover tightly and cook 15
minutes longer, or until rabbit is
tender and mussels have opened.
Serve paella directly from pan.

Opposite: Basque Paella (p. 63)
Overleaf: Herbed Crepes with Mexican Chicken
(p. 69)

RICE WITH POULTRY
AND MEAT

DIRTY RICE

SERVES 4

INGREDIENTS

4 tablespoons olive oil
8 ounces (240 g) chicken livers,
chopped
8 ounces (240 g) chicken
gizzards, chopped
1 large onion, chopped
1 small green bell pepper,
chopped
3 stalks celery, chopped
2 cloves garlic, chopped
salt and freshly ground pepper
to taste
1 cup (225 g) rice
2 cups (480 mL) chicken stock
6 scallions, chopped
¼ cup (7 g) chopped Italian
parsley

"Dirty rice" is not an appealing name, but indeed the chicken livers and gizzards give the rice a brown tinge. Here is a version I had in New Orleans. It makes a wonderful side dish with fried chicken.

Heat 2 tablespoons olive oil in a large heavy skillet and sauté livers and gizzards until lightly brown.

In a separate skillet, heat remaining oil and sauté onion, pepper, celery and garlic for 5 minutes. Add vegetables to liver and gizzards, season with salt and pepper and cook over low heat for 30 to 40 minutes or until gizzards are almost tender. Add rice and chicken stock. Bring mixture to boil, reduce heat, cover and cook for 10 minutes. Add scallions and parsley and cook 10 minutes longer.

In a wok or large skillet heat 1 tablespoon oil over high heat. Sauté garlic and ginger for 1 minute. Add green pepper and carrot and stir-fry for 2 minutes. Mix in scallions, remove from wok and set aside. Wipe out wok and heat remaining 2 tablespoons peanut oil. Pat chicken cubes dry, add to hot oil and stir-fry for 3 minutes. Return vegetables to wok. Stir in hoisin sauce and chicken stock and stir-fry for 2 minutes. Sprinkle with peanuts and serve over rice.

Note: If hoisin sauce is unavailable, substitute equal parts of peanut butter and catsup.

HOISIN CHICKEN AND RICE

SERVES 6

INGREDIENTS

3 tablespoons peanut oil, divided
2 cloves garlic, minced
1 tablespoon minced fresh ginger
1 green bell pepper, cut into 1-inch (2.5-cm) squares
2 carrots, thinly sliced
4 scallions, chopped
1 pound (450 g) chicken breast, cut into 1-inch (2.5-cm) cubes
¼ cup (60 mL) hoisin sauce, or more to taste
¼ cup (60 mL) chicken stock
½ cup (60 g) dry-roasted peanuts
3 cups (225 g) hot cooked rice

CHICKEN CASSEROLE CON QUESO

SERVES 6

INGREDIENTS

3 cups (225 g) cooked rice,
cooled
3 cups (525 g) cooked chicken,
cut into chunks
1 cup (115 g) sliced celery
1½ cups (175 g) grated
Monterey Jack cheese, divided
½ cup (120 mL) salsa
½ cup (120 mL) sour cream
⅓ cup (80 mL) mayonnaise
salt and freshly ground pepper
to taste
1 clove garlic, minced
hot pepper sauce to taste
½ cup (60 g) crumbled corn chips

A good buffet dish must be delicious and easy to put together; it also should not require a knife. This one wins on all three counts.

Preheat oven to 350°F (180°C). In a large bowl lightly toss together rice, chicken, celery, ¾ cup (90 g) cheese and salsa.

In a small bowl stir together the sour cream, mayonnaise, salt, pepper, garlic and hot pepper sauce. Add to rice mixture and blend well. Turn mixture into a shallow buttered 1½-quart (1.5-L) baking dish. Sprinkle with remaining cheese and corn chips. Bake for 30 minutes or until cheese is bubbly.

Here's a nice company dish that can be assembled in advance and refrigerated until guests arrive. Put the crepes in the oven while you serve margaritas.

To make crepes, combine milk, eggs, flour, salt and butter in a blender or processor and blend until smooth. Stir in cilantro, chives, chilies, basil and rice. Refrigerate for 1 hour. Batter should have the consistency of heavy cream; if necessary, thin with a small amount of milk.

Heat an 8-inch (20-cm) skillet and brush with oil. Stir batter and pour ¼ cup (60 mL) into pan. Quickly tilt pan so that batter covers bottom completely. Cook over medium heat until golden brown on underside. Loosen edge, turn and cook until lightly browned on other side. Remove crepe and cool on wire rack. Repeat with remaining batter, stacking crepes between pieces of waxed paper.

To make chicken, heat 2 tablespoons oil in a large skillet or Dutch oven and sauté onion, green pepper and

HERBED CREPES WITH MEXICAN CHICKEN

SERVES 8

HERBED CREPES

1½ cups (360 mL) milk

3 eggs

1¾ cups (210 g) all-purpose flour

salt to taste

2½ tablespoons (38 g) butter, melted

1 tablespoon chopped fresh cilantro

1 tablespoon snipped fresh chives

2 tablespoons finely chopped canned green chilies

1 tablespoon chopped fresh basil

1 cup (75 g) cooked rice, cooled

MEXICAN CHICKEN

4 tablespoons vegetable oil, divided
1½ cups (175 g) chopped onion
1 small green bell pepper, diced
1 tablespoon minced garlic
3 cups (525 g) uncooked chicken
cut into 1-inch (2.5-cm) cubes
3 tablespoons chili powder
1 tablespoon dried oregano
1 teaspoon ground cumin
½ teaspoon dried
red pepper flakes
2½ cups (600 mL) chicken stock
1 6-ounce (180-g) can tomato paste
salt to taste
2 cups (150 g) cooked rice
1 cup (240 mL) sour cream,
for garnish
1 avocado, peeled, seeded and
diced, for garnish

garlic until tender but not browned. Remove and set aside. Add remaining 2 tablespoons oil to pan and sauté chicken for 5 to 10 minutes. Add chili powder, oregano, cumin and red pepper flakes and stir to coat chicken. Add onion mixture, chicken stock, tomato paste and salt and stir well. Bring to boil, reduce heat and simmer 1 hour.

To assemble crepes, preheat oven to 350°F (180°C). Spoon 2 tablespoons rice and 2 tablespoons chicken mixture across center of each crepe. Overlap two opposite sides over filling. Arrange crepes seam side down in greased shallow baking dish. Cover with foil and bake for 15 to 20 minutes. To serve, top each crepe with a dollop of sour cream and diced avocado.

Chinese wonton wrappers are used instead of pasta dough for these ravioli.

Melt butter in a skillet and sauté mushrooms and shallot until all moisture evaporates. Add turkey, rice, tarragon, cream cheese, salt and pepper and blend well.

Separate wonton wrappers. Place a tablespoon of turkey mixture on center of half the wrappers. Brush remaining wontons with egg. Place on turkey-covered wontons. Press together around edges, beginning at the center to force out any air.

Bring chicken stock and water to simmer in a skillet. Lower ravioli into liquid, a few at a time, and cook about 4 minutes or until ravioli become translucent. Remove, drain on paper towels and set aside.

Reduce cooking liquid over high heat to 1 cup (240 mL). Add heavy cream and reduce to 1½ cups (360 mL). Arrange ravioli on a serving platter and pour sauce over. Sprinkle with Parmesan cheese.

TURKEY RAVIOLI

SERVES 6

INGREDIENTS

1 tablespoon (15 g) butter
1 cup (70 g) finely chopped mushrooms
1 shallot, finely chopped
1 cup (175 g) finely chopped cooked turkey
1 cup (75 g) cooked rice
1 tablespoon chopped fresh tarragon
3 ounces (90 g) cream cheese, softened
salt and freshly ground pepper to taste
1 pound wonton wrappers (about 50)
1 egg, beaten
4 cups (1 L) chicken stock
2 cups (480 mL) water
1 cup (240 mL) heavy cream
½ cup (60 g) freshly grated Parmesan cheese

ARROZ CON PATO

SERVES 4

INGREDIENTS

2 tablespoons olive oil
1 duckling, cut into quarters,
remove excess fat
½ cup (60 g) chopped onion
2 plum tomatoes, seeded,
chopped
1 small green bell pepper,
chopped
2 fresh jalapeño peppers,
seeded, chopped
2 cloves garlic, crushed
¼ cup chopped cilantro
2 cups (480 mL) chicken stock
salt and freshly ground pepper
to taste
1 cup (225 g) long-grain rice
½ cup (115 g) peas, fresh or
frozen
¼ cup (60 mL) beer

Arroz con pollo is a favorite Spanish dish, sort of a paella made without seafood. This spinoff substitutes duck (pato) for the chicken.

In a large flameproof casserole heat oil and brown duck on all sides.

Remove and set aside. Add onion, tomato, green pepper, jalapeño peppers and garlic to casserole and sauté until onion is limp.

Add cilantro to vegetables with duck, chicken stock, salt and pepper. Cover and simmer for 30 minutes.

Skim off fat. Pour off liquid from casserole and add more chicken stock, if necessary, to make 2 cups (480 mL). Return liquid to casserole and add rice and peas. Stir, cover and simmer for 20 minutes or until rice is almost tender. Add beer and cook an additional 7 to 8 minutes or until duck is tender.

Opposite: Country French Stew (p. 79)

Osso Buco, which means "bone with a hole," is a traditional Milanese dish. It is most often served with saffron-flavored golden risotto.

Have butcher cut the meatless end from each shank; the remaining portion should be cut into 2-inch (5-cm) slices. Tie each piece around the middle with a piece of string.

Dredge shanks in flour. Heat 2 tablespoons olive oil in a skillet and brown shanks on all sides. Add wine and cook until it evaporates. Set aside.

In a separate pan heat remaining 2 tablespoons olive oil and sauté onion, chopped garlic, carrot and celery for 10 minutes. Add crushed tomatoes, lemon peel strips, thyme, basil, bay leaf, salt and pepper. Cover pan and simmer for 15 minutes. Cover veal shanks with tomato sauce and simmer for 35 to 40 minutes. Turn veal shanks over, cover and cook for another 30 minutes or until meat is tender. Remove string and discard lemon peel and bay leaf.

OSSO BUCO WITH GREMOLATA AND RISOTTO ALLA MILANESE

SERVES 6

INGREDIENTS

4 meaty veal shanks, cut into
2-inch (5-cm) slices
flour for dredging
4 tablespoons olive oil, divided
1 cup (240 mL) dry white wine
(preferably Italian)
1 large onion, chopped
2 cloves garlic, chopped
2 carrots, peeled and chopped
2 stalks celery, chopped
2 cups (480 mL) canned crushed
tomatoes
2 strips lemon peel (without any
pith)
¼ teaspoon dried thyme
3 to 4 fresh basil leaves, torn
1 bay leaf
salt and freshly ground pepper to
taste
1 teaspoon grated lemon peel
1 clove garlic, minced
¼ cup (7 g) chopped Italian parsley

Opposite: Osso Buco with Gremolata and Risotto Milanese

RISOTTO ALLA MILANESE

SERVES 6

INGREDIENTS

½ cup (120 g) butter
2 whole shallots, minced
1½ cups (340 g) arborio rice
4 cups (1 L) hot chicken stock
⅛ teaspoon saffron, crumbled
2 tablespoons dry white wine
(preferably Italian)
½ cup (60 g) freshly grated
Parmesan cheese
salt and freshly ground pepper
to taste

To make gremolata, combine grated lemon peel, minced garlic and chopped parsley. Sprinkle over veal shanks and serve.

To make risotto, melt butter in a medium saucepan and sauté shallots until soft but not brown. Slowly stir in rice and sauté until it is a light golden brown.

Add ½ cup (120 mL) chicken stock, stirring constantly. When stock is absorbed, stir in another ½ cup (120 mL). Dissolve saffron in 2 tablespoons hot stock and add to rice. Continue stirring in stock, ½ cup (120 mL) at a time, until rice is al dente and creamy; total cooking time will be about 20 minutes. Stir in wine, then cheese. Season to taste with salt and pepper.

Need something different for a covered-dish supper? This Middle Eastern-inspired rice and lamb combination will have everyone asking for the recipe.

In a large skillet heat 1 tablespoon oil over medium heat and cook lamb with salt, cumin, coriander, nutmeg and hot pepper until lamb is brown. Remove meat mixture and set aside.

Heat remaining tablespoon of oil in same skillet and cook onion, bell pepper, sugar, turmeric, cinnamon and chili powder until onion is soft, about 3 to 5 minutes. Stir in rice.

Preheat oven to 350°F (180°C). Spread half the rice mixture in the bottom of a buttered shallow 3-quart (3-L) baking dish. Top with meat mixture and spread remaining rice mixture in a smooth layer on top; do not pack down. Sauté sliced onion in butter in same skillet until soft but not brown. Spread evenly over rice mixture. Cover dish and bake for 20 minutes.

SAVORY LAMB AND RICE

SERVES 6

INGREDIENTS

2 tablespoons olive oil, divided
12 ounces (360 g) lean ground lamb
1 teaspoon salt
½ teaspoon ground cumin
½ teaspoon ground coriander
⅛ teaspoon nutmeg
⅛ teaspoon crushed hot pepper flakes
1 cup (115 g) chopped onion
½ cup (60 g) chopped red bell pepper
1 teaspoon brown sugar
½ teaspoon turmeric
½ teaspoon cinnamon
½ teaspoon chili powder
3 cups (225 g) cooked rice (cooked in chicken stock)
1 medium onion, thinly sliced
1 tablespoon (15 g) butter

APPLE PORK PIE

SERVES 4 TO 6

INGREDIENTS

1 pound (450 g) lean ground
pork
2 cups (200 g) sliced, peeled
Granny Smith apples
1 cup (75 g) cooked rice
½ teaspoon dried thyme
2 tablespoons firmly packed
brown sugar
4 fresh sage leaves or ½ teaspoon
dried sage
salt and freshly ground pepper
to taste
2 tablespoons (30 g) butter
1½ cups (340 g) biscuit mix
¼ cup (60 mL) milk
¼ cup (60 mL) apple cider
1 cup (240 mL) sour cream
2 tablespoons horseradish, or to
taste

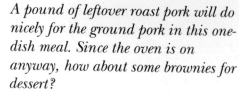

A pound of leftover roast pork will do nicely for the ground pork in this one-dish meal. Since the oven is on anyway, how about some brownies for dessert?

Cook pork in a skillet until it changes color, breaking it apart with a fork or wooden spoon. Drain well.

Preheat oven to 400°F (200°C). Layer apple slices in a buttered deep 10-inch (25-cm) baking dish. Combine pork, rice, thyme, brown sugar, sage, salt and pepper and mix well. Cover apples with pork mixture.

In a medium bowl combine biscuit mix, milk and cider. Stir to combine and knead 15 times on a lightly floured surface. Roll out into an 11-inch (27.5-cm) circle and place over pork mixture. Tuck in sides to cover apples completely. Cut 3 vents in top. Bake for 20 minutes or until crust is golden brown.

To make horseradish dressing, combine sour cream and horseradish. Serve with pie.

Here's a colorful side dish to serve with grilled chicken or to take along on a picnic.

Cook bacon in a skillet until crisp. Remove bacon, drain and crumble; set aside. Sauté kielbasa, onion, celery, bell peppers and garlic in bacon fat for 7 to 8 minutes, stirring occasionally. Add wild rice, molasses, salt and pepper and stir until hot and well combined. Sprinkle with reserved bacon before serving.

WILD RICE AND SAUSAGE

SERVES 6

INGREDIENTS

4 ounces (120 g) thick-sliced bacon
1 pound (450 g) smoked kielbasa, sliced ½ inch (1 cm) thick
1 small onion, chopped
1 stalk celery, chopped
½ green bell pepper, chopped
½ red bell pepper, chopped
1 clove garlic, chopped
1½ cups (340 g) wild rice, cooked according to package directions
2 tablespoons molasses
salt and freshly ground pepper to taste

JAMBALAYA

SERVES 6

INGREDIENTS

2 tablespoons olive oil
½ cup (60 g) chopped onion
½ cup (60 g) chopped celery
½ green bell pepper, diced
2 cups (480 mL) canned crushed
tomatoes
¾ teaspoon dried thyme
salt and pepper to taste
1 bay leaf
¼ teaspoon cayenne pepper
2 tablespoons dry white wine
3 cups (225 g) hot cooked rice
8 ounces (250 g) chicken breasts,
cooked, cubed
8 ounces (250 g) smoked sausage,
cooked, sliced
8 ounces (250 g) ham, cubed
8 ounces (250 g) shrimp, cooked,
peeled
8 ounces (250 g) cod or haddock,
cooked, cubed
hot pepper sauce

Jambalaya is a Cajun Creole favorite that mixes several meats and fish with rice in a tomato-based sauce. The dish always begins with the "holy trinity"—onions, celery and green pepper.

In a large saucepan heat olive oil and cook onion, celery and green pepper until soft but not brown. Add tomatoes, thyme, salt, pepper, bay leaf, cayenne pepper and wine and simmer 30 minutes. Remove bay leaf.

Preheat oven to 350°F (180°C). In a large bowl combine rice, chicken, sausage, ham, shrimp and fish. Add tomato sauce and stir gently. Turn into a lightly greased shallow 3-quart (3-L) baking pan. Bake for 15 to 20 minutes or until thoroughly heated through and all liquid is absorbed. Serve with hot pepper sauce.

The flavors of Provence—thyme, rosemary and bay leaf—make this a typically peasant-style stew/soup. Feel free to add a few fresh green peas or slices of zucchini to the pot.

Heat 1 tablespoon oil in a stockpot and cook chicken and pork until browned on all sides. Remove and set aside.

In same pot heat remaining oil and cook mushrooms, onion and celery until vegetables are tender, stirring occasionally.

Add browned meat, rice, tomatoes, wine, thyme, rosemary and bay leaf and bring to boil. Reduce heat, cover and simmer for 45 minutes or until meat is tender, stirring two or three times.

Stir in kielbasa, beans, parsley, salt and pepper and simmer for 15 minutes longer. If stew is too thick, thin with stock or additional crushed tomatoes.

FRENCH COUNTRY STEW

SERVES 8

INGREDIENTS

2 tablespoons olive oil, divided
8 ounces (240 g) boneless chicken breasts
8 ounces pork cutlet, cubed
1 cup (60 g) sliced mushrooms
1 large onion, chopped
2 stalks celery, chopped
½ cup (115 g) long-grain rice
1½ cups (360 mL) canned crushed tomatoes
1 cup (240 mL) dry white wine or chicken stock
1 tablespoon chopped fresh thyme or 1 teaspoon dried thyme
½ teaspoon dried rosemary, crumbled
1 bay leaf
8 ounces (240 g) smoked sausage such as kielbasa
1 cup (240 g) cooked cannellini beans
½ cup (15 g) chopped parsley

INDONESIAN RICE WITH CURRY SAUCE

SERVES 12

INGREDIENTS

4 tablespoons olive oil, divided
1 cup (115 g) chopped onion
½ red bell pepper, chopped
½ green bell pepper, chopped
2 cloves garlic, chopped
2½ cups (565 g) converted rice
6 cups (1.5 L) chicken stock
1 tablespoon curry powder,
or to taste
juice of 1 lime
¼ cup (30 g) all-purpose flour
2 14-ounce (420 g) cans
unsweetened coconut milk
¼ cup (90 g) peanut butter
1 tablespoon grated fresh ginger
3 cups (525 g) coarsely chopped
cooked chicken breast

GARNISH

chutney, chopped roasted peanuts,
fried plantains, chili peppers,
chopped toasted coconut, raisins

Canned unsweetened coconut milk can be purchased in health food and specialty food stores. To make your own, grate the peeled meat of a medium coconut and combine with the coconut liquid and sufficient water or milk to make 1 quart (1 L). Bring slowly to boil. Cool, then strain mixture and discard grated coconut.

In a large pot heat 2 tablespoons olive oil and sauté onion, peppers and garlic until onion is limp. Stir in rice and stock and bring to boil. Reduce heat, cover and simmer for 20 minutes or until rice is tender.

Heat remaining 2 tablespoons olive oil in a skillet, add curry powder and cook until bubbly. Remove from heat. Add lime juice and flour and blend well. Return to heat, slowly add coconut milk and cook, whisking constantly, until mixture thickens. Whisk in peanut butter and ginger.

To serve, mound rice in center of dish and arrange chicken around it. Spoon curry sauce over rice. Serve garnishes in separate dishes.

Opposite: Indonesian Rice with Curry Sauce
Overleaf: Peach Ambrosia Rice Custard (p. 87)

RICE IN BREADS
AND DESSERTS

HONEY 'N' DATE MUFFINS

MAKES 12

INGREDIENTS

2 cups (240 g) all-purpose flour
1 tablespoon baking powder
½ teaspoon salt
1 cup (75 g) cooked brown rice
⅔ cup (160 mL) milk
¼ cup (90 g) honey
⅓ cup (80 g) butter or
margarine, melted
1 egg, well beaten
½ cup (60 g) chopped dates

Cooked brown rice adds interesting texture to these breakfast muffins.

Preheat oven to 400°F (200°C). In a medium bowl combine flour, baking powder and salt.

In a separate bowl combine rice, milk, honey, butter, egg and dates. Add dry ingredients and stir just until combined; batter will be lumpy. Spoon batter evenly into 12 greased or paper-lined muffin cups. Bake for 18 to 20 minutes or until golden brown. Remove from pan immediately, running a knife around the edge to loosen, if necessary. Serve warm.

Rice seems an unlikely ingredient for bread, but it lends an interesting texture to this quick bread. The dough can also be rolled out and cut into biscuits; in this case, bake them for 12 to 15 minutes.

Heat 1 tablespoon butter in a small skillet and sauté onion until transparent. Set aside to cool.

Preheat oven to 400°F (200°C). In a large bowl combine flour, baking powder and salt. Cut in shortening with a pastry blender or fingers until mixture resembles coarse meal. Combine egg and milk and add to flour mixture, blending with a fork until just moistened. Stir in onion, rice, rosemary and cheese. Spread dough in a greased 8-inch (20-cm) round baking pan. Brush with remaining butter. Bake for 35 minutes or until toothpick inserted in center comes out clean. Serve immediately.

CHEESE AND ONION RICE BREAD

SERVES 8

INGREDIENTS

3 tablespoons (45 g) butter, melted
¾ cup (85 g) chopped onion
1½ cups (180 g) all-purpose flour
1 tablespoon baking powder
½ teaspoon salt
⅓ cup (80 g) solid white shortening
1 egg, slightly beaten
½ cup (120 mL) milk
1 cup (75 g) cooked rice, cooled
1 cup (115 g) grated swiss cheese
1 teaspoon chopped fresh rosemary

RICE WAFFLES WITH HONEY-MAPLE SYRUP

MAKES 8 WAFFLES

INGREDIENTS

1 cup (120 g) all-purpose flour
2 teaspoons baking powder
2 tablespoons sugar
pinch of salt
2 egg yolks, beaten
1 cup (240 mL) milk
2 tablespoons (30 g) melted
butter
1 cup (75 g) cooked rice
2 egg whites, beaten stiff
½ cup (180 g) honey
½ cup (120 g) maple syrup
1 teaspoon cinnamon
2 tablespoons (30 g) butter

Rice waffles freeze well and can be reheated in the toaster.

In a medium bowl combine flour, baking powder, sugar and salt. Toss lightly with a fork. In a small bowl combine egg yolks, milk and melted butter. Add wet ingredients to dry ingredients and mix until smooth. Gently fold in rice and beaten egg whites. Bake in a hot waffle iron following manufacturer's instructions.

To make syrup combine honey, maple syrup, cinnamon and butter in a small saucepan and bring to simmer. Serve warm over waffles.

Calas are deep fried puffs of rice-infused batter. They're sold on the streets of the French Quarter in New Orleans.

In a medium bowl whisk eggs and add salt, sugar, nutmeg, cinnamon and baking powder. Add vanilla and flour and whisk until well blended. Gently fold in rice. Cover batter and let stand for 20 minutes.

Heat oven to 250°F (120°C). In a deep saucepan heat oil to 360°F (180°C). Drop rounded tablespoons of batter into oil and fry until golden brown, turning once. Drain on paper towels. Keep calas warm in the oven. Sprinkle with confectioners' sugar while still warm and once again just before serving.

CALAS

MAKES 24

INGREDIENTS

2 eggs
½ teaspoon salt
¼ cup (60 g) sugar
¼ teaspoon nutmeg
¼ teaspoon cinnamon
1 tablespoon baking powder
2 tablespoons vanilla extract
1 cup (120 g) all-purpose flour
2 cups (150 g) cold cooked rice
vegetable oil for deep-frying
confectioners' sugar

ST. JOSEPH'S FRITTELLE

MAKES ABOUT 24

INGREDIENTS

2¼ cups (540 mL) milk
1 cup (225 g) long-grain rice
⅓ cup (80 g) sugar
dash salt
¼ cup (45 g) golden raisins
¼ cup (30 g) pine nuts
2 tablespoons finely chopped
candied citron, optional
2 eggs
¼ cup all-purpose flour
1 teaspoon baking powder
2 tablespoons marsala
1 tablespoon grated orange peel
vegetable oil for deep-frying
confectioners' sugar

The feast of St. Joseph, on March 19, is a favorite Florentine holiday. One food for the day is frittelle, *rice balls studded with raisins and pine nuts.*

In a medium saucepan combine milk, rice, sugar and salt and bring to simmer. Cover and cook over low heat until milk is absorbed, about 30 minutes. Stir in raisins, pine nuts and citron. Let cool, and chill.

In a small bowl whisk together eggs, flour, baking powder, marsala and orange peel. Combine with rice mixture.

Pour vegetable oil into a deep sauce-pan to a depth of 2 inches (5 cm) and heat to 375°F (190°C). Drop dollops of batter the size of a walnut into hot oil and fry until golden brown, turning once; do not crowd. Drain frittelle *and sprinkle with confectioners' sugar while still warm. Sprinkle with sugar again just before serving.*

Fresh July peaches make this dessert a natural, but drained canned or frozen sliced peaches make an adequate substitute.

Preheat oven to 350°F (180°C). In a medium bowl combine rice, eggs, salt, sugar, vanilla, lemon peel and milk. Turn into a buttered shallow 2-quart (2-L) baking dish. Set dish into a pan of hot water filled to within 1 inch (2.5 cm) of top. Bake for 30 minutes. Stir mixture with spoon. Bake 30 minutes longer or until a knife inserted near the center comes out clean. Remove from water bath.

In a medium bowl combine peaches, lemon juice, liqueur and coconut. Toss lightly and chill until serving time.

Arrange peach mixture on top of custard. Serve warm or at room temperature.

PEACH AMBROSIA RICE CUSTARD

SERVES 8

INGREDIENTS

1½ cups (115 g) cooked rice
5 eggs, beaten
¼ teaspoon salt
½ cup (120 g) sugar
2 teaspoons vanilla extract
1½ teaspoons grated lemon peel
3½ cups (850 mL) milk
2 cups (450 g) peeled fresh peaches, sweetened to taste
1 tablespoon fresh lemon juice
2 tablespoons peach schnapps or brandy
1 cup (120 g) shredded sweetened coconut

RASPBERRY RICE ELEGANCE

SERVES 8

INGREDIENTS

1 15-ounce (450 g) container ricotta
¾ cup (180 mL) half-and-half
2 eggs
⅔ cup (160 g) sugar, divided
1½ teaspoons vanilla extract, divided
½ teaspoon cinnamon
2 cups (150 g) cooked rice
1 cup (150 mL) sour cream
¼ cup (60 g) seedless raspberry jelly
1 tablespoon cornstarch combined with 1 tablespoon water
1 10-ounce (300-g) package frozen raspberries

With a snazzy raspberry sauce, this homey rice pudding is elegant enough for a fancy dinner party.

Preheat oven to 325°F (165°C). In a medium bowl beat together ricotta, half-and-half, eggs, ⅓ cup (80 g) sugar, 1 teaspoon vanilla and cinnamon. Stir in rice. Spoon mixture into a buttered 9-inch (23-cm) springform pan. Bake until set, 45 to 60 minutes.

Combine sour cream with remaining sugar and vanilla. Spread over rice mixture and bake 5 minutes longer. Cool, then refrigerate until chilled.

Melt jelly in a small saucepan. Stir in cornstarch mixture and cook, stirring constantly, until mixture is clear and thickened. Add berries and cook over low heat, stirring frequently, until berries are thawed. Transfer to a bowl, cover and chill.

To serve, cut rice custard into wedges and spoon a few tablespoons sauce over each wedge.

Opposite: Raspberry Rice Elegance

Humble rice pudding is gussied up with Grand Marnier sauce and rosy pear slices.

Mix marmalade and Grand Marnier in a small bowl and set aside for 45 minutes.

Combine rice, 2 tablespoons sugar and 1½ cups (360 mL) milk in a medium saucepan and bring to boil. Reduce heat and simmer until milk is absorbed, stirring often. Remove from heat. Stir in butter and vanilla.

Soften gelatin in ¼ cup (60 mL) water. Combine 4 tablespoons sugar and ⅓ cup (80 mL) milk in small saucepan and bring to simmer. Beat egg yolks with remaining ⅓ cup (80 mL) milk and stir into sugar/milk mixture. Cook over low heat until mixture coats back of spoon; do not boil. Add softened gelatin and stir to dissolve. Remove from heat.

Add gelatin mixture and marmalade mixture to rice mixture. Cool. Fold in whipped cream. Spoon into 8 individual molds. Cover and chill for 6 hours.

Opposite: Creamy Rice Pudding with Poached Pears

CREAMY RICE PUDDING WITH POACHED PEARS

SERVES 8

INGREDIENTS

¼ cup (60 g) orange marmalade
2 tablespoons Grand Marnier or other orange liqueur
1½ cups (340 g) short-grain rice
6 tablespoons sugar, divided
1½ cups (360 mL) milk
1 tablespoon (15 g) butter
1½ teaspoons vanilla extract
1 envelope unflavored gelatin
¼ cup (60 mL) water
⅔ cup (160 mL) milk
2 egg yolks
¾ cup (180 mL) heavy cream, whipped
1½ cups (360 g) sugar
⅛ teaspoon ground cardamom
3 cups (720 mL) hearty red wine
3 fresh pears, peeled and cored with stem intact
orange peel slivers for garnish

For poached pears, combine 1½ cups (360 g) sugar, cardamom and wine in a nonaluminum medium saucepan and bring to boil. Add pears. Reduce heat, cover and poach gently until pears are tender. Remove pears and boil wine mixture until reduced to 1 cup (240 mL). Refrigerate pears and wine sauce.

To serve, unmold each pudding onto dessert plate. Pour sauce around pudding. Slice pears thinly lengthwise and fan slices around pudding. Garnish with orange peel slivers.

Chocolate lovers especially will adore this creamy frozen dessert.

Combine rice, sugar, chocolate, salt, milk and eggs in large saucepan and cook over low heat until mixture just begins to bubble, stirring constantly. Cool. Add cream and extracts. Chill well. Pour mixture into ice cream maker and freeze according to manufacturer's directions.

CHOCOLATE RICE FROZEN CUSTARD

SERVES 8

INGREDIENTS

1½ cups (115 g) cooked rice
1 cup (240 g) sugar
4 ounces (120 g) unsweetened
chocolate, melted
pinch of salt
3 cups (720 mL) milk
2 eggs, beaten
2 cups (480 mL) heavy cream
1 teaspoon orange extract
1 teaspoon chocolate extract
1 teaspoon vanilla extract

AMARETTO RICE CHEESECAKE

SERVES 12

INGREDIENTS

1 cup (115 g) chocolate cookie
crumbs
1 cup (120 g) finely chopped
almonds
2 tablespoons sugar
1 teaspoon cinnamon
⅓ cup (80 g) butter, melted

2 cups (150 g) cooked rice
1 15-ounce (450 g) container
ricotta cheese
8 ounces (240 g) cream cheese,
softened
1 cup (240 g) sugar
4 eggs
⅓ cup (80 mL) amaretto liqueur

1 cup (240 mL) sour cream
1 tablespoon sugar
1 tablespoon amaretto liqueur
grated semisweet chocolate for
garnish
toasted almond slices for garnish

Ricotta is generally associated with dense Italian-style cheesecake, but here it's lightened with cream cheese, flavored with amaretto and garnished with chocolate and almonds.

To prepare crust, combine crumbs, almonds, sugar, cinnamon and butter. Press mixture onto bottom and 1 inch (2.5 cm) up sides of ungreased 9-inch (22.5-cm) springform pan.

Preheat oven to 350°F (180°C). To prepare filling, combine rice and ricotta in food processor until smooth. Beat cream cheese and sugar until light and fluffy. Add eggs one at a time, beating well after each. Blend in amaretto and rice mixture. Pour filling into prepared crust. Bake for 1 hour. Remove cheesecake; retain oven temperature.

To prepare topping, blend sour cream, sugar and amaretto. Spoon over cheesecake and bake for 10 minutes. Cool, then refrigerate overnight. Garnish with chocolate and almonds.

INDEX

Marie Bianco is a food writer with Newsday. *She is the author of four other Barron's books,* 32 Seafood Dishes, 32 Fabulous Cookies, Wild About Potatoes, *and* Wild About Salads.